JAN -- 2016

W9-AUS-744

Investigating
Sedimentary Rocks

DES PLAINES PUBLIC LIBRARY
1501 ELLINWOOD STREET
DES PLAINES, IL 60016

Miriam Coleman

PowerKiDS
press.

New York

Published in 2016 by The Rosen Publishing Group, Inc.
29 East 21st Street, New York, NY 10010

Copyright © 2016 by The Rosen Publishing Group, Inc.

All rights reserved. No part of this book may be reproduced in any form without permission in writing from the publisher, except by a reviewer.

First Edition

Editor: Sarah Machajewski
Book Design: Katelyn Heinle

Photo Credits: Cover kojihirano/Shutterstock.com; p. 4 Sarah Jessup/Shutterstock.com; p. 5 Wildnerdpix/Shutterstock.com; p. 6 (igneous rock) Horia Bogdan/Shutterstock.com; p. 6 (metamorphic rock) meunierd/Shutterstock.com; p. 7 crydo/Shutterstock.com; p. 8 Dchauy/Shutterstock.com; p. 9 Jane Rix/Shutterstock.com; p. 11 De Agostini Picture Library/De Agostini/Getty Images; p. 13 (conglomerate) sonsam/Shutterstock.com; pp. 13 (breccia), 18 Tyler Boyes/Shutterstock.com; p. 13 (sandstone) Alexlukin/Shutterstock.com; p. 13 (siltstone) Harry Taylor/Dorling Kindersley/Getty Images; p. 13 (shale) Sarah2/Shutterstock.com; p. 14 (coal) SeDmi/Shutterstock.com; p. 14 (chalk) Richard Newstead/Moment/Getty Images; p. 15 (rock salt) LatitudeStock - Dennis Stone/Gallo Images/Getty Images; p. 15 (gypsum) BIOPHOTO ASSOCIATES/Photo Researchers/Getty Images; p. 16 De Agostini Picture Library/De Agostini Picture Library/Getty Images; p. 17 Doug Lemke/Shutterstock.com; p. 19 BGSmith/Shutterstock.com; p. 20 steve estvanik/Shutterstock.com; p. 21 Visuals Unlimited, Inc./John Cornell/Visuals Unlimited/Getty Images; p. 22 Arthur Tilley/Stockbyte/Getty Images.

Coleman, Miriam, author.
  Investigating sedimentary rocks / Miriam Coleman.
    pages cm. — (Earth science detectives)
  Includes bibliographical references and index.
  ISBN 978-1-4777-5951-6 (pbk.)
  ISBN 978-1-4777-5952-3 (6 pack)
  ISBN 978-1-4777-5950-9 (library binding)
  1. Sedimentary rocks—Juvenile literature. 2. Earth sciences—Juvenile literature. 3. Geology—Juvenile literature. 4. Earth (Planet)—Juvenile literature. I. Title.
  QE471.C654 2015
  552.5—dc23
                          2014029744

Manufactured in the United States of America

CPSIA Compliance Information: Batch #WS15PK: For Further Information contact Rosen Publishing, New York, New York at 1-800-237-9932

CONTENTS

SOLVING MYSTERIES IN THE ROCKS

Scientists are detectives. They gather **evidence** and search for clues that can help them solve mysteries. Geologists are scientists who study what Earth is made of and how it was formed.

Geologists know rocks contain many clues about how old Earth is and how it has changed over time. If an area of land was once underwater, we can learn that from the rocks. Rocks can tell us where glaciers once cut through mountains or where **volcanoes** once blew up. Rocks can even tell us what animals lived in an area and what the weather was like long ago.

What clues about Earth do these rocks contain?

These **layers** of rock are a record of a time before people were even on Earth.

THREE TYPES OF ROCKS

Geologists sort rocks into three main types: igneous, metamorphic, and sedimentary. Each kind is formed in a different way and holds different clues about what happens above and below Earth's surface.

Igneous rocks form when melted rock inside the earth rises, cools, and hardens. Metamorphic rocks are formed when very high heat and **pressure** change the minerals in the rock. In this book, we'll focus on sedimentary rocks, the most common rocks on Earth's surface.

igneous

metamorphic

CLUE ME IN

Rocks are made of minerals, which are nonliving matter found in nature. Quartz is a mineral commonly found in rocks.

sedimentary

The three different kinds of rocks each teach us something different. They can tell us what's inside Earth, what forces act upon Earth, and in the case of sedimentary rocks, what kinds of things were once found on Earth.

WHAT IS A SEDIMENTARY ROCK?

Sedimentary rocks are made of layers of sediment that collect on a surface and **compact** to form hard rock. Sediments can be small pieces of rock, sand, mud, or dirt. They can even be bits of plants and animals. Almost all of Earth's surface is covered in sediments and sedimentary rocks.

Sedimentary rocks are like time capsules. Each layer formed at a different point in time. Layers are often different colors and thicknesses. The layers' age, color, and thickness are clues about what was happening on Earth when they formed.

More layers of rock will be **revealed** as the water running over them wears them down over time.

The layers in sedimentary rocks are also called strata.

HOW DOES SEDIMENTARY ROCK FORM?

The forming of sedimentary rocks begins with weathering. Rain, ice, snow, and wind break down rocks. The tiny parts of rock that are weathered away become the sediments that form sedimentary rock. Moving water, such as rivers, often carries sediments to the bottom of lakes or oceans.

As more sediments are deposited, or dropped, they build up in layers. Over time, the weight of the new layers creates pressure and compacts the bottom layers. The pressure from the new sediments squeezes air and water out of the layers below. Then, the minerals in the sediments form crystals, which bind the sediments together and make rock.

CLUE ME IN

Weathering is when rocks are worn away or broken down into tiny pieces because of rain, ice, wind, and more. This is also called erosion.

A LOOK AT LITHIFICATION

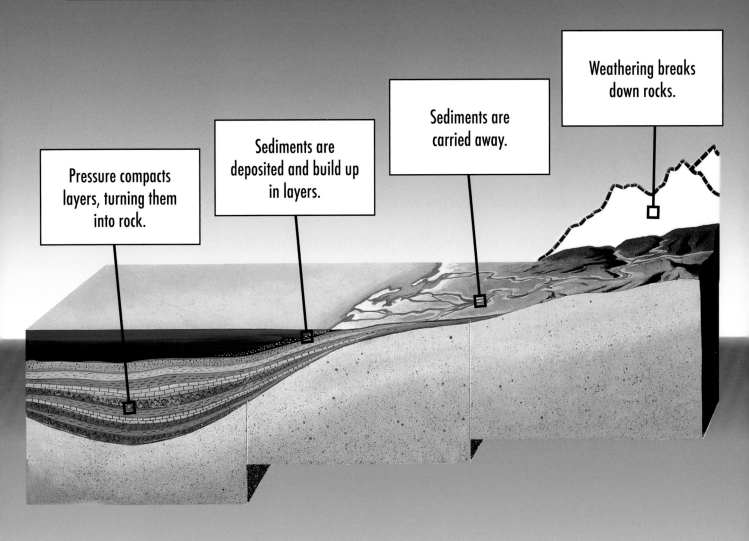

Pressure compacts layers, turning them into rock.

Sediments are deposited and build up in layers.

Sediments are carried away.

Weathering breaks down rocks.

The process of turning sediments into stone is called lithification (lih-thuh-fuh-KAY-shun). Lithification takes millions and millions of years.

CLASTIC SEDIMENTARY ROCKS

Scientists split sedimentary rocks into groups based on how they form. Clastic sedimentary rocks are formed from sediments created by the weathering of existing rocks. The sediments' size and shape are clues about what matter was in the area where the rock formed and how far away the sediments were from where the rock is now.

Bits of rock get smaller and smoother the farther they travel from where they broke off. Clastic rocks made of big pieces with sharp points are called breccia. The sediment that made those rocks probably didn't travel too far. Rocks made of big, rounder pieces are called conglomerates. Their sediment likely came from places farther away.

CLUE ME IN

Sandstone is made up of rock pieces the size of grains of sand. Sandstone can be found where there were once beaches or deserts.

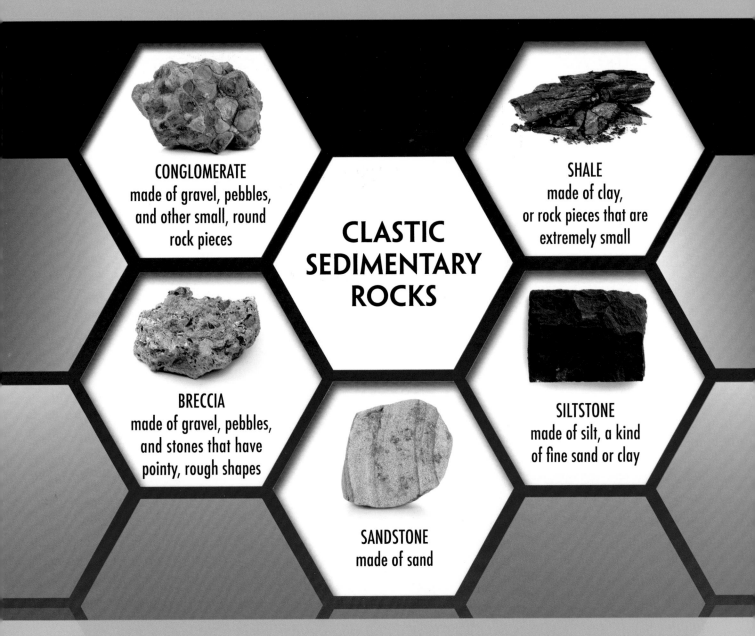

CONGLOMERATE
made of gravel, pebbles,
and other small, round
rock pieces

SHALE
made of clay,
or rock pieces that are
extremely small

CLASTIC SEDIMENTARY ROCKS

BRECCIA
made of gravel, pebbles,
and stones that have
pointy, rough shapes

SILTSTONE
made of silt, a kind
of fine sand or clay

SANDSTONE
made of sand

Clastic rocks are found all over the world. They're made of sediments that could've come from anywhere, such as high mountains or ancient beaches.

The word "organic" describes something that comes from living matter, such as plants or animals. In organic sedimentary rocks, the sediments come from the remains of plants and animals that lived long ago. Coal is an example of an organic sedimentary rock. It formed from the matter of plants that grew in swamps 300 million years ago. Chalk is a sedimentary rock made from the shells of tiny sea animals.

CLUE ME IN

Gypsum is a mineral that appears when a large body of water **evaporates**. As the water evaporates, it leaves behind gypsum that was **dissolved** in it.

coal

chalk

Chemical sedimentary rocks form when minerals dissolve in water and then **precipitate** from it. Rock salt, for example, forms when water evaporates and leaves salt, which had been dissolved in it, behind.

gypsum

rock salt

Geologists know rock salt is a sign that a lake or other body of water once existed and has dried up.

WHAT KIND OF ROCK IS IT?

Geologists look at rocks to find clues about what they're made of and how they were formed. A rock's **texture** is a major clue that tells a lot. Geologists look at the rock's grains. The millions of grains could be pieces of different kinds of rocks or different kinds of minerals, or they could all be the same.

Geologists also look at the shape of the grains to see whether they're rounded and smooth or sharp and pointy. They look to see whether all the grains in the rock are the same size or many different sizes, too.

rock grains

Sediments can come from anywhere and be anything, which is why the layers of sedimentary rocks can be different colors and sizes.

FINDING FOSSILS

Fossils are the hardened remains of plants and animals that lived long ago. They're often found in sedimentary rocks.

An ancient creature became a fossil if its remains were buried under sediments before weather and other animals destroyed them. If the remains included bones, the minerals in the bones were **replaced** by ones that made the remains strong enough to last over time. If sedimentary rock didn't form to protect ancient remains, we would never know about some of the plants and animals that lived long ago.

shale with a fossilized leaf

CLUE ME IN

Clams, coral, fish, and insects are just some examples of fossils commonly found in sedimentary rocks.

Geologists look at how old rock layers are in order to find out when the animals or plants buried in them lived. It's one way we can use sedimentary rock to learn about Earth's past!

WAVES AND BEDS

Geologists look at the tiny pieces in sedimentary rocks, but looking at the big picture is important, too. Large sedimentary rocks bear marks and patterns that show how they were formed. You can see stripes of different colors and sizes in some sedimentary rocks, with the oldest layers at the bottom and the newest on top.

Sometimes rocks contain layers that tilt up or down instead of lying flat like the main layers. This is called cross bedding. It's a sign that water or wind once carried the sediment in different directions.

This sedimentary rock contains a pattern that looks like waves. Seeing the pattern helps us imagine the water that once washed over this rock, even though the water is no longer there.

CLUES ALL AROUND US

Sedimentary rocks are found everywhere on Earth. From the beautiful stripes of the Grand Canyon to a hunk of clastic rock found in a river, sedimentary rocks contain records of Earth's history that date back millions of years.

Learning how to read the clues in these rocks—about how they were formed and what they're made of—can teach us much about how Earth has been shaped. The next time you find a rock lying on the ground, take a closer look. What can it tell you about your world?

GLOSSARY

chemical: Matter that can be mixed with other matter to cause changes.

compact: To press firmly together.

dissolve: To mix a solid completely into a liquid.

evaporate: To change from a liquid to a gas.

evidence: Facts, signs, or information that proves something to be true.

layer: One thickness lying over or under another.

precipitate: To cause a dissolved substance, such as a mineral, to be deposited in a solid form.

pressure: A force that pushes on something else.

replace: To take the place of.

reveal: To show.

texture: In geology, the size of a mineral's crystals or grains in rocks.

volcano: An opening in Earth's surface through which hot, liquid rock sometimes flows.

INDEX

WEBSITES

Due to the changing nature of Internet links, PowerKids Press has developed an online list of websites related to the subject of this book. This site is updated regularly. Please use this link to access the list: www.powerkidslinks.com/det/sedi

24